MONITORING AND EVALUATING

a practical guide for school governors

David Marriott

Adamson Publishing

© David Marriott 2004

Published by Adamson Publishing Ltd
Akeman House, High Street, Stretham,
Ely, Cambridgeshire CB6 3JQ
tel: 01353 649238 fax: 01353 648184
e-mail: info@adamsonbooks.com
www.adamsonbooks.com

ISBN 0-948543-21-3

British Library Cataloguing in Publication Data
A catalogue record for this book is available from the British Library

Cover design by Geoff Shirley

Printed and bound by Black Bear Press Ltd, Cambridge, England

CONTENTS

The author

David Marriott is Head of Governor Support in Wiltshire. He has worked in education all his life – as a secondary school teacher, head of faculty and deputy head prior to his current post.

An experienced governor himself, David provides advice, guidance and training for primary and secondary governors. He has written for the *Times Educational Supplement*, *Governors' Agenda* and *School Governor Update*, and his first book, *The Effective School Governor*, was published by Network Educational Press in 1998.

INTRODUCTION

How properly to monitor and evaluate has continued to top the list of issues that perplex and confuse governors for the best part of a decade.

This is not surprising, given that there is so much contradictory advice available from a number of sources, especially Ofsted and the DfES, and that the advice itself has changed several times since 1995.

Few governors fail to understand that monitoring and evaluation lie at the heart of their roles, but many are unsure how to carry out these activities. How are they meant to do them? What are they supposed to monitor and evaluate? When should they do it? Are monitoring and evaluation one and the same thing? What if they step on the toes of the head and teachers?

ACHIEVING THE IMPOSSIBLE

One of the most common symptoms of being a governor is guilt. It's the result of never having enough time to do all the things that governors feel they are expected to do. With monitoring and evaluation there is a real danger that governors could try to monitor and evaluate everything that moves. And if so, they will inevitably fail. We have to think through what this means. We need to see that we should focus only on the core activities that add value to our contribution to the school. It may mean stopping doing some of the things we do now and certainly will mean not trying to do the impossible.

However, there is a very significant gap between what is actually possible and what those responsible for national education legislation, policy and practice expect governors to do. That's not a reason to give up, of course, but to concentrate on those aspects of our work that will have the greatest impact on our key purpose, which is to help our school to provide the best possible education for all its pupils.

There is now a heavy emphasis on school self-evaluation, not least in the Ofsted Framework (full title: *Inspecting Schools: Framework for inspecting schools*, Ofsted, 2003) and Handbook (three titles: *Handbook for Inspecting Nursery and Primary Schools, Handbook for Inspecting Secondary Schools* and *Handbook for Inspecting Special Schools and Pupil Referral Units*, Ofsted, 2003). The better the school's self-evaluation, the more confident inspectors are that the school is effective. A governing body, as a core element of the leadership and management of the school, plays an important part in this. It follows, then, that monitoring and evaluation are key elements in governors' work.

Although this is essentially a practical guide, with examples and advice based on experience, monitoring and evaluation can only be made to make sense in the context of theory, that of the three main roles we have as governors (strategic, critical friend and accountability).

Some governors are very familiar and comfortable with the school's processes of strategic and development planning, monitoring and evaluation. But for many others, these things can appear daunting and seem to lie beyond their "amateur" knowledge and capabilities. They aren't easy but doing them is less of a challenge than it may seem. Part of the problem, as so often in governorship, is the language. The words imply complex and sophisticated concepts. It sounds as though you have to be a bit of an expert to talk about them, let alone do them!

YOU'RE ALREADY DOING IT!

The reality is different. Most people perform the core activities of governance all the time in their personal lives as well as in any professional context. They just don't always use the same terms to describe their actions. For example, most of us manage domestic budgets. We plan family events that can be very complicated, like weddings. We weigh up the pros and cons of sending our children to particular schools. Dealing with crises, doing several things at once, changing our arrangements in the light of circumstances – they're part and parcel of our daily lives.

Governors bring "the precious light of ordinariness" to schools. The trouble is, they don't always recognise the skills they have or how they could be applied to the school. The professional jargon gets in the way.

Let's take the example of a family holiday abroad to see how we might make better use of governors' everyday skills and knowledge. How does going on holiday relate to planning, monitoring and evaluation?

First, before you go away, you need to find out what each member of the family wants from the holiday and plan to meet everyone's needs and expectations as far as you can. At school, this relates to consultation with teachers, head and governors about priorities for the year ahead and ensuring that contributions from all members of the school community are included as far as possible. With a family holiday we need to decide where to go, when to go and how to get there. The corresponding school processes involve agreeing a shared vision, setting a timescale and deciding the main actions in the plan. The family has to decide what it can afford and adjust the plans as necessary. The school equivalent is identifying likely costs and linking actions to the available budget.

You're still not ready to go, though. There are still all the practical arrangements, such as checking passports, buying travel guides and maps, arranging for necessary injections and so on. In the school context, we're putting the detail into the plan and thinking through the resource needs. You have to make sure the house is secure while you're away, cancel the milk, and arrange accommodation for the pets, etc. Similarly, we have to ensure the maintenance of school – keeping everything going on a daily basis – while we focus on development.

OK. You're nearly there! Now there's just packing and cleaning the house. At school, we're ensuring we have all we're likely to need to carry out the fine detail of the plan and establishing a clear baseline before the plan starts.

Once you're on holiday, you might organise different activities on different days and keep checking that everyone's happy and doing what they wanted to do. You'll be keeping an eye on the weather and people's health, changing plans accordingly, as necessary, and, of course, keeping an eye on the money. You'll send postcards and take photos or make a video.

In the school the corresponding activities involve focusing on the different elements of the plan at different times. We monitor activities by different people and check that planned actions are going ahead, making adjustments in view of changed circumstances. We keep an eye on the budget. People make brief reports on school activities and record key events and developments.

All good things must come to an end, however. Unpacking and doing the laundry, collecting the pets and reading the mail await you on your return. You get the photos developed and show them (or the video) to friends and family, giving out the presents you bought while you were away. Let's hope you can pay off your credit cards and change any surplus currency while you plan the next holiday in the light of what you have experienced on this one.

The school process consists of taking stock at the end of the development period, evaluating what went well and what could be improved; reporting on progress and celebrating success. We review and adjust the budget before starting the next plan, following our assessment of what happened with the last one.

With a little encouragement and a helpful analogy, even the most deferential and self-effacing governors can be helped to see how their everyday experience and knowledge can be brought to bear on a variety of school governance tasks. But don't push these comparisons too far – being a governor is not really one long holiday!

1. WHY SHOULD WE MONITOR AND EVALUATE?

The classic definition of the three key roles of a governing body was first outlined in *Governing Bodies and Effective Schools* (Ofsted/BIS/DFE, 1995):

- to provide a strategic view
- to act as a critical friend
- to ensure accountability.

The *Handbook for Inspecting Nursery and Primary Schools* (Ofsted, 2003) now defines the governing body's three roles as to:

- provide a strategic direction for the work and improvement of the school
- support, monitor and evaluate the effectiveness of the school
- hold the school to account for the standards achieved and the quality of education.

This is a more helpful definition, since it fleshes out the roles and makes a more logical sequence. It also indicates that monitoring and evaluation are central to the governors' role.

MONITORING FOR SCHOOL IMPROVEMENT

How governors can "support, monitor and evaluate the effectiveness of the school" is the central concern of this book. There is a difference between effectiveness and improvement. For most schools effectiveness looks to the future, our shared vision of how good things could be. Our school is probably producing the desired outcomes in a number of areas but could be better in others. Even where it is already effective, it may be possible to develop things further. Improvement, then, is the process we use to make the school more effective.

Without a clear view of what an effective school looks like, you cannot improve or evaluate how far you have improved. Fortunately, you don't have to work out for yourself what an effective school looks like, as there is a huge body of research evidence from which you can draw.

One of the best definitions says that a school is effective if it:

- promotes progress for all its pupils beyond what would be expected given consideration of initial attainment and background factors
- ensures that whatever pupils achieve is at the highest level
- enhances all aspects of pupil achievement and development
- maintains these positive effects consistently from year to year.

(Louise Stoll and Peter Mortimore, *School Effectiveness and School Improvement*, Institute of Education, University of London, Viewpoint no. 2, June 1995)

This useful definition starts from the concept that it is commonly called "added value", which is the difference the school makes to a child's education, and goes on to add further challenges. It especially recognises that there are many forms of achievement beyond the SATs results in English, Maths and Science and that effectiveness has to be maintained over a long period of time.

RECOGNISING AN EFFECTIVE SCHOOL

Long-term international research has defined eleven key features of effective schools:

- participatory leadership
- shared vision and goals
- teamwork
- a learning environment
- emphasis on teaching and learning
- high expectations
- positive reinforcement
- monitoring and enquiry
- pupil rights and responsibilities
- learning for all
- partnerships and support.

(Stoll and Mortimore, 1995)

The writers go on to describe these in more detail. For example, it is explained that for a school to be effective in terms of "monitoring and enquiry" there would have to be *monitoring of pupil performance and evaluation of school performance*. The improvement processes leading to this would include

- setting, monitoring and evaluating success criteria
- classroom research techniques used by teachers
- ongoing review and necessary adaptation.

So, we know what an effective school looks like. We monitor and evaluate our progress towards becoming as effective as possible. What that means in practical terms is the focus of the rest of this book.

2. WHAT SHOULD WE MONITOR AND EVALUATE?

Although monitoring and evaluation are very similar and can and do overlap, they are not the same thing. Difficulties arise because in a lot of what has been written about them, few if any clear distinctions have been made. In much of Ofsted's literature and in many of its reports on schools – especially before 2001 – monitoring was used as a generic term when often what was meant was evaluation.

In *Making It Better: Improving school governance* (2002), Ofsted finally provided helpful definitions:

Monitoring: checking that actions are being or have been taken

Evaluating: measuring the effect of the actions on the school's performance.

This clarification should make governors' lives easier. Monitoring appears as a very simple, quick task, while evaluation is the more complicated and, arguably, important of the two, especially for governors. Evaluation then emerges as the thing you should focus on.

OFFICIAL GUIDANCE

A further complication is that during the last decade or so many lists of what governors should monitor and evaluate have been published in books, leaflets and guidance documents. Two prominent instances of these come, as you would expect, from Ofsted and the Department for Education and Skills.

Ofsted view of what governors should monitor and evaluate

In *Making It Better* Ofsted emphasised that it was the school that governors were responsible for monitoring and evaluating, which means, in practice:

- monitoring and evaluating the school's action plan
- monitoring the curriculum
- visiting the school.

Ofsted's is a short list, obviously, although monitoring the curriculum, as we'll see later on, could be a huge task. However, it is worth bearing in mind that the publication was aimed mainly at governors in schools with serious weaknesses or in special measures, so it refers primarily to monitoring and evaluation in that context.

In 2002, the *National Training Programme for School Governors* (DfES) included a longer list under the heading "What should be monitored and evaluated?":

- National Curriculum assessments and tests and/or secondary examination results
- quality of teaching and learning
- pupils' independence as learners
- pupil attendance
- pupils' behaviour, attitudes and self-esteem
- pupil exclusions
- pupil involvement in extra-curricular activities
- number of applications for admission
- destinations of school leavers
- leadership and management
- school ethos/culture
- staff morale, attendance and commitment
- home-school communication
- views and involvement of parents, pupils and the community
- information on the school's curriculum, staffing and budget
- the learning environment.

DfES guidance on monitoring and evaluation

In a follow-up section, the training programme says:

Governors need to be part of a whole school self-evaluation strategy ... Governors do not need to try to keep track of everything that a school does ... the headteacher is responsible for ensuring the quality of teaching. Governors are not expected to make professional judgements when they observe lessons. They do need to contribute to the process of evaluation, considering summaries of evidence gathered by the head and the staff.

Considering that the advice from these two bodies is different, it's no wonder that governors are baffled! If we tried to follow it all, ignoring the worst of the contradictions, we could spend every waking hour monitoring and evaluating and never get anywhere near completing the task.

To hang on to our sanity, we have to be very cool and objective about the task. The simple fact is that nobody in authority really knows for certain what governors should monitor and evaluate.

USING THE ANNUAL REPORT TO PARENTS AS GUIDANCE

As discussed in the last chapter, you could start from where you're trying to get to. Monitoring and evaluation provide the information you need in order to see how far you've travelled towards achieving effectiveness. A more practical approach that still focuses on effectiveness is to ask "What are we accountable for?"

The annual report to parents is a helpful guide, bearing in mind that its function is for governors to discharge their accountability to parents for the performance of the school. You have to monitor and evaluate the various subjects that have to be included in the report, otherwise you would not have the information that you are supposed to publish. This is as follows.

School performance data

The statistical data needed for the annual report should be easy enough to collate from existing sources and records – and is mostly provided by the headteacher. Starting with school performance data he or she can provide:

- rates of pupils' authorised and unauthorised absence
- the school's National Curriculum assessment results at all Key Stages and results at GCSE and GNVQ
- the school's targets for Key Stage 2 and 3 assessments.

The head should also be able to account for how teachers' professional development impacts on teaching and learning.

The clerk can provide us with details of the governing body membership, including the name and address of the chair and the clerk.

Policies and plans

This leaves us, working in partnership with the head, to account for policies and plans:

- information about the implementation of the governing body's policy on pupils with special educational needs (SEN) and any changes to the policy during the last year
- a statement on progress in implementing the action plan drawn up following an inspection
- the accessibility plan covering future policies for increasing access to the school by those with disabilities, and steps being taken to prevent disabled pupils being treated less favourably than other pupils.

Budget

We're responsible for the budget, in the form of a financial statement.

School environment

We need to account for certain aspects of the school environment:

- information about school security
- details of existing facilities to assist access to the school by pupils with disabilities.

So, this analysis of the main threads of the annual report gives us a basic list of things we need to monitor and evaluate.

Summary of indications from the annual report to parents

Evidence from the requirements of the annual report to parents indicates that governing bodies should monitor and evaluate the following:

- school performance data
- policies and plans
- the budget
- the school (or learning) environment.

USING INSPECTION REQUIREMENTS AS GUIDANCE

We also have to take account of what Ofsted inspectors are going to want from us. This will give us a few more items to add to the basic list.

The inspection Framework and Handbook place a heavy emphasis on school self-evaluation.

Ofsted recognises the importance of school self-evaluation as a continuous process that is complemented from time to time by external inspection. Self-evaluation makes an important contribution to inspections. It provides the school and the registered inspector [*sic*: the official term now is "lead inspector"] with a means of ensuring that inspection covers matters of potential significance to the school.

Inspection takes account of or contributes to school self-evaluation by using the school's summary of its self-evaluation as the basis for discussion between the registered inspector and the headteacher and, where possible, governors of the school, when the inspection is being planned. The quality and use made of school self-evaluation is also a good indication of the calibre of management. Evidence of how effectively schools undertake self-evaluation and the use they make of it helps inspectors to evaluate the quality of management in the school and the capacity of the school to improve.

New Framework for School Inspection, The Education Network, Policy Briefing, 2003

According to this, any monitoring or evaluation carried out by a governing body only makes sense as part of whole school self-evaluation; this is also in line with advice given in the National Training Programme for School Governors. As you will see in Chapter 7, there are many resources available to governors to support self-evaluation. One of the best places to start on whole school self-evaluation is with the S3 and S4 forms which have to be completed prior to an Ofsted inspection. Form S3 is a checklist of statutory responsibilities, and working through it as a governing body highlights the need to have in place and keep under review some key policies. (Monitoring and evaluating policies are covered in detail in chapter 4.) However, it is S4 that really focuses on self-evaluation.

Using the Ofsted Form S4 for school self-evaluation

It is now common for schools to complete the S4 form on an annual basis as their main self-evaluating activity, and governors are increasingly brought into this analysis. The questions asked by S4 focus on overall school effectiveness, its record of achievement, teaching and learning, links with parents and the community, leadership and management.

The questions require the respondent to grade the school on a seven-point scale from 1, excellent, to 7, very poor. Each question is followed by two or three sub-questions such as "How do you know?", "What are your notable strengths?" and "What are the main priorities for improvement?" Governors are not expected to know all the answers immediately but they should have an input into some of them. In exploring the answers to the rest, with the head and other staff, the governing body will be fulfilling its responsibility to evaluate the effectiveness of the school overall.

In practice, it may be that the work of completing the form is done with the head and/or leadership team by the chair, a committee or other sub-group of the full governing body, but all need to know what the completed S4 says about the school. If the form is simply completed by the senior management and given to the governing body, you are missing a vital opportunity to become active in your evaluative role.

Inspection of governance

During inspection governors are now under the microscope.

The onus is on the governing body to evaluate itself as part of the overall process of school self-evaluation, so we need to add this to our shopping list of what we need to monitor and evaluate.

> Inspectors must evaluate and report on the governance of the school, assessing the extent to which the governing body:
>
> - helps shape the vision and direction of the school
>
> - ensures that the school fulfils its statutory duties, including promoting inclusive policies in relation to special educational needs, race equality, disability and sex
>
> - has a good understanding of the strengths and weaknesses of the school
>
> - challenges and supports the senior management team.
>
> *Handbook for Inspecting Nursery and Primary Schools*, Ofsted, 2003

Summary of indications from school self-evaluation

In summary by looking at our various accountabilities we can work out that, as part of whole school self-evaluation, we need to monitor and evaluate relevant aspects of:

- school performance data

- policies and plans

- the budget

- the school (or learning) environment

- our own performance as a governing body.

THE HEADTEACHER'S REPORT

We will address each of the areas in the above list in the subsequent chapters. Before doing so, though, it's important to remind ourselves that one of the most important sources of the information we need in order to monitor and evaluate the main aspects of our school is under our noses at governing body meetings: the headteacher's report to the governing body.

The headteacher's written report to the governing body should be presented at least termly, if not at every meeting of the full governing body. The main purpose of the report is to give governors the information they need to fulfil their statutory responsibilities, including monitoring and evaluating all the areas listed above.

While there is guidance on the recommended content of such reports, practice varies considerably between schools, and new heads tend to use the model provided by the previous head. The DfE in 1996 listed the following items that the report should "generally include":

- plans or issues requiring review or decision

- update on the head's fulfilment of management functions

- progress made with the school development/improvement plan

- information on the achievements of pupils, teachers and other staff

- information about expenditure with reference to the school's budget.

It then added a list of other possible topics:

- pupil statistics
- staff statistics
- visitors
- curriculum
- school policies
- inspections
- private funds
- premises
- special events
- parent-home liaison.

Guidance on Good Governance, DfE, 1996

Clearly the remit of the report covers a lot of topics. There is always a danger, then, that the head includes too much in the report for fear of not sharing sufficient information with the governors. Governors may end up daunted by the sheer volume of information.

Starting from these lists, it's a good idea to review from time to time with the head what the report should include *in your context*. Two key questions need to be addressed:

- What do the governors *really* need to know?
- What does the head *really* need to tell the governors about?

If you can agree this between you, you're likely to end up with a much punchier, more practical document than you may be used to receiving. For example, you might note that information on special events is already perfectly well covered in other documents you receive. Budgetary information will probably be part of the finance committee's regular reports. Seek out and remove any information that is duplicated elsewhere. Your target must be to achieve a report that you can *use*, not just receive – and that's as much your responsibility as it is the head's.

Sharpening the focus

It's more than reasonable for the head to expect all governors to have read the report before the meeting and to have come prepared to ask challenging questions. That way, you avoid the shambolic speed-reading and lack of questions that too often characterises this part of the agenda. Most heads spend a lot of time and thought on their report and it's very disheartening when it becomes obvious that some of the governors haven't bothered to read it in advance.

You should look critically at the way the information is provided. For example, if you're to engage with the information rather than simply receive it, perhaps the head could include some questions – or boxes inviting the governors to write in their own questions to be asked at the meeting when the report is discussed. For example, reports sometimes include a long list of training courses attended by the staff. So what? OK, it helps us to know that staff development is taking place but how appropriate is it? More importantly, what impact is the training having in the classroom?

The report is one of the best ways you have as a governor to know what's going on in the school. There are other sources of data and evidence, as we shall see in subsequent chapters, but you should always start from the head's report. If it doesn't tell you what you need to know in order to do your job, work with the head to improve it.

3. HOW WELL ARE WE DOING? SCHOOL PERFORMANCE

PERFORMANCE MANAGEMENT

Performance management was introduced in schools in 2000, replacing an unsatisfactory appraisal system. Governors became responsible for setting objectives for the headteacher and reviewing the extent to which they were achieved at the end of the year, and also for approving a policy for the performance management of the rest of the teaching staff.

Working from evidence about the school's performance, the head, the governors appointed to review the head's performance and an external adviser agree a small number of objectives for the year ahead, especially in relation to pupil performance and leadership and management. The objectives should be SMART, i.e. specific, measurable, achievable, relevant and time-constrained. Progress towards the objectives should be monitored through the year and evaluated at the next annual review meeting with the external adviser.

Success factors

Performance management of the headteacher is one of the ways in which governors can monitor and evaluate an important element of school performance, although the confidentiality surrounding the publication of the outcomes of the process can hamper the governing body's collective knowledge of how well the head is doing.

Of course, the school is bigger than the head, so you cannot rely on performance management alone to judge school performance. As an approach, though, it gives you a lot of important pointers as to how to do it successfully. The success of the performance management system is due to several features which we can apply to other aspects of our monitoring and evaluation role:

- *A policy and a procedure*
  The statutory basis of performance management ensures that each school has a robust policy and procedure for the process.

- *The precision of the objectives*
  SMART objectives are not always possible in every aspect of the school's work but the smarter the objectives the better! They define from the outset how you will assess them when the time comes.

- *A cycle*
  Ideally, the annual performance management cycle synchronises with the school improvement cycle, so one process informs the other.

- *Evidence*
  As is discussed later in this chapter, there is a lot of statistical and other data on which to draw. Evidence is crucial to monitoring and evaluation.

Evidence

Put simply, monitoring is the process of gathering evidence and evaluation is making judgements of what the evidence tells you.

- *A meeting*
  The formal meeting provides a proper context and procedure for the evaluation. It ensures all participants play an appropriate part along agreed guidelines, including the recording of the outcomes.

- *An external professional*
  Perhaps the most important factor is the presence and participation of the trained adviser, who lends an objective view and can ensure fair play in achieving an acceptable outcome.

MONITORING AND EVALUATING PERFORMANCE

Making It Better (Ofsted, 2001) describes how one governing body came face to face with weaknesses in its monitoring and evaluation practice:

Two of the most important functions of governors are their monitoring and evaluation of the school's performance, yet in many schools these are often the weakest areas of their work.

"By the end of the meeting we had checked and discussed with the headteacher that the school development plan was being implemented as planned; the school budget had sufficient funds for the rest of the school year; and it had been shown that the pupils' most recent national test results had improved on those for last year. Obviously, we felt we were monitoring and evaluating the school. As it turned out, we later learned that although the school development plan was being implemented, nobody was checking to see what impact the work was having; with a predicted fall in the number of pupils in the school the budget was likely to go into deficit if we did not lose a teacher; and although our test results were better than last year, they were really low compared to similar schools. In effect, we simply did not have a firm grip on what was going on at all!"

These comments summarise neatly some of the key problems faced by governors when monitoring does not lead to evaluation. The DfES provides additional advice on what to monitor and on how to progress to evaluation:

Governing bodies will need to monitor progress, but are not responsible for collecting monitoring data themselves. Instead they should agree arrangements with their headteacher.

Working strategically, governors should then use any monitoring evidence [i.e. statistical data relating to pupil and school performance] to review and evaluate progress against any targets set to see whether a policy is working or needs changing. The head can suggest arrangements for monitoring and evaluating particular requirements and policies.

Governing bodies should make sure they get enough information (from the headteacher) to allow them to check on their school's achievements and progress, over time and in comparison with similar schools.

Roles of Governing Bodies and Head Teachers, DfEE, 2000

Monitoring the monitoring

Are these pieces of advice consistent with one another? The DfES seem to be saying that governors should restrict themselves to evaluation rather than monitoring, especially in relation to school performance. Ofsted appear to give equal weight to both monitoring and evaluation by governors. Remember, though, that although much of what it says is of general relevance, *Making It Better* is specifically published for governors in schools that have failed their inspection. The book goes on to give a further view of monitoring, which shows that Ofsted and the DfES are in reality singing from the same hymn sheet here:

Effective governors use...results...to compare the school's performance with the results of recent years, of national and LEA averages, and with similar schools.

Moreover:

Governors need to know who among the staff is responsible for the day-to-day monitoring, and for checking the agreed action is taking place. It is helpful if a governor is linked with each key issue, and checks that monitoring is showing whether action has or has not been taken.

This is in effect stating that the governors' role is more to do with *monitoring the monitoring* rather than the initial monitoring itself, which is the responsibility of school staff.

Questions governors should ask when monitoring pupils' attainment

How do our results compare overall and by subject with those of previous years? (Are they rising, holding steady, or falling? Have we met our targets?)

How do they compare with national standards?

How do they compare with similar schools?

How well do different groups of pupils progress? (Key stages, year groups, gender, ethnicity, special educational needs, high attainers?)

How do different subjects compare with each other?

Making It Better, Ofsted, 2001

One could take issue with Ofsted over the word "monitoring" in this context in the box above, since it seems to be much more about evaluation of the school's achievements. However, the advice is good and provides governors with the challenging questions to ask.

Who should be asking these questions? The chair should take a lead, though a committee could be the appropriate forum, feeding back to the main governing body, and all governors should be prepared to ask them. The answers are crucial in informing the process of developing the next school improvement plan, so all governors need to know what they are – and why they are as they are – and what is needed to improve.

DATA IN SCHOOLS

Schools generate a lot of evidence of performance through teachers' customary monitoring processes of assessment, marking, moderation and standardisation. This is supplemented by the results of national tests (commonly called SATs) and other raw data produced by external assessment. LEA advisers also produce monitoring and evaluation reports on their schools, though this information is not always made available to governors. Each school has access to an Autumn Package, of which a key part is the PANDA report, and this provides a fuller context within which the results may be interpreted.

The table on the next page shows what data is commonly available to schools. Your school may receive more than this, depending on local factors and policy.

There is no shortage of information – but what should governors see and what are they to make of it?

Ofsted report

The report of an inspection is the fullest and most objective report you are likely to receive as a governor. The full report goes into considerable detail about all aspects of the school, while the summary condenses the main findings to about four sides of A4. The summary, especially, is an excellent starting point for any governor wishing to get an overview of how good their school is. If there are particular areas in which he or she is interested then the full report will put the flesh on the bones.

Its main weakness is that it has a limited shelf life, being a snapshot of a particular period in the life of the school. The older it is, the less useful it is. Schools prepare for the inspection, so the report should be a picture of the school at its best and normal performance may be less good than the report portrays (though stress may have the opposite effect). At the same time, the report may not take fully into account some of the issues affecting the school. Staff absence can distort the picture; for example, if an excellent teacher was replaced by an uncertain supply teacher on the day of the inspection, then that particular subject may be deemed to be worse than it really is.

Whilst there is an "Ofsted-speak" designed to minimise ambiguities and standardise the way judgements are expressed in different reports, Ofsted reports are not difficult to interpret. They are designed to be read by staff, parents, governors and the wider community.

Autumn Package

The Autumn Package is freely available and published on-line annually on www.standards.dfes.gov.uk by the DfES using national pupil performance data based on the results of statutory National Curriculum tests taken at the four Key Stages. At Key Stage 4, the tests take the form of the GCSE and the GNVQ. In the words that used to appear on the website, the information contained provides practical help:

> It can be used to examine aspects of a school's performance against all schools nationally or to a group of similar schools. It also allows the user to investigate performance at school and pupil level and help answer the following questions a school might have:

- How well have we done?
- What could we have done differently?
- What can we expect in the future?
- What more should we aim to achieve?

School performance data

Data	Published by	When/frequency	Recipients	What does it tell us?
Ofsted report	Ofsted	Roughly every four–six years	Governors, Leadership team, Teachers, Parents, LEA, Local community	*Effectiveness of the school* 1. How successful is the school? 2. What should the school do to improve? *Standards achieved by pupils* 3.1 How high are standards achieved in the areas of learning and subjects of the curriculum? 3.2 How well are pupils' attitudes, values and other personal qualities developed? *Quality of education provided by the school* 4. How effective are teaching and learning? 5. How well does the curriculum meet pupils' needs? 6. How well are pupils cared for, guided and supported? 7. How well does the school work in partnership with parents, other schools and the community? *Leadership and management of the school* 8. How well is the school led and managed? 9. How good is the quality of education in areas of learning and subjects? 10. What is the quality of other specified features?
Autumn Package	Ofsted and QCA	Annually: autumn term	Head	National summary results, value-added information and benchmark information. This allows schools to understand what progress they are making, compare the progress made by individual pupils with progress made by other pupils with similar prior attainment, and compare their performance with similar schools.
PANDA *NB technically, it is part of the Autumn Package*	Ofsted	Annually: autumn term	Head, Chair (only by asking head for it!), LEA	Performance and Assessment Data. The contents of each PANDA report are confidential between Ofsted, the school, and the Local Education Authority, although schools are free to disseminate the information as they see fit.
SATs results	QCA	Annually: autumn term	Head, Teachers, Governors, Parents, Pupils, LEA	Teacher Assessment and national test results in core subjects at the end of Key Stages 1–3
GCSE, AS and A level results	Various exam boards	Annually: August	Students, Head, Teachers, Parents, Governors, LEA	The achievement of each student in all the subjects they have studied (secondary schools only)
LEA adviser report	LEA adviser	Could be termly; at least annually	Head, LEA, Chair (usually)	Report on specific aspects of the school
School-generated data	School	Throughout the year	Head, Staff, Governors (?)	Practice varies from school to school. Could include reading scores, Cognitive Ability Test (CAT) results, value-added data
Attendance data	School	Possibly termly; at least annually	Head, Staff, Governors, LEA	Record of pupil non-attendance (authorised and unauthorised)
Exclusions data	School	Possibly termly; at least annually	Head, Staff, Governors, LEA	Record of pupil exclusions, both fixed-term and permanent

Throughout, a school should be looking for instances of where performance in their school is different to expectations, whether better or worse. This can then inform classroom practices and school strategy in order to raise pupil performance.

The document is split into three sections and contains **national summary results, national value-added information** and **national benchmarking information**.

- National summary results allow for comparisons of a school's performance against national averages and trends. A school will be able to calculate where the greatest differences between the two occur. This provides a starting point in identifying the main issues for the school.

- National value-added information enables a school to: identify which pupils they should be concerned with, to evaluate the school's effectiveness over the Key Stages for different types of pupils and to set expectations for pupils entering the Key Stage. The section provides two tools based on matched pupil level data: Value-added Line Graphs and Progress Charts. Schools can use Value-added Line Graphs, for example, to evaluate pupils' progress between Baseline Assessment and KS1. The graphs enable schools to compare the progress of their pupils with progress achieved nationally while taking into account prior performance. The Progress Charts provide information to support schools in raising their expectations of pupil achievement and can be used in setting realistic but challenging targets.

- National benchmarking information allows a school to make more detailed comparisons nationally and with other similar schools.

The website also contains information about the **Pupil Achievement Tracker (PAT)**. This computer software allows schools and LEAs to import and analyse their own pupil performance data against national performance data published in the Autumn Package.

Clearly, some of this statistical data and analysis is very sophisticated. The reference in the guidance on its use is to "schools" – which may or may not include the governing body. The important thing from the governors' point of view is to know that all this data is available for schools to use, so that they can ask the head and other staff what use they make of it. Ideally, the head and staff will share with governors annually how they have used the Autumn Package for school improvement.

If the school is making no use of it whatsoever, the governing body should be concerned, since it is a very valuable resource, and the chair of governors should ask the head why. If the head is a little insecure in using data, some training or advice might be necessary; most LEAs provide these.

For schools with a small cohort of pupils (less than roughly 25) in any year group the Autumn Package data is not as useful as their own knowledge of each individual pupil, but this is not a reason for the school to make no use of it at all.

The PANDA report

The school's PANDA (Performance and Assessment data) report, which is published electronically by Ofsted each autumn, gives information about the previous school year's pupil performance in national tests and public exams. Although not published simultaneously with it, it is technically part of the Autumn Package. Whereas all other data in the Autumn Package is about schools and pupils nationally, the PANDA report tells you about *your* school and *your* pupils.

The contents of the PANDA report are confidential between Ofsted, the school, and the LEA. The reports give an overview of the school's performance in relation to other schools using data from Ofsted, the DfES and the Qualifications and Curriculum Authority (QCA). The reports are designed for use as a management tool to help schools in the development and implementation of plans to raise standards. They are not part of the public reporting of the school's performance.

Throughout the PANDA, the school's performance is shown in comparison with national averages, and, using the national benchmarks in the Autumn Package, in comparison with other schools in similar contexts as defined by free school meal statistics (for socio-economic status) and with the prior attainment of the pupils tested.

Obtaining the PANDA

You can download your PANDA from the website (www.ofstedpandas.guide.net) providing you have the school's six digit unique reference number (URN) and this year's password. These details are supplied in a letter from Ofsted to the school each year. You could also telephone or e-mail the PANDA helpline (020 7421 6840/6633 or raihelpdesk@ofsted.gov.uk).

Information is given in three different ways: as graphs, charts and prose, with grades. It's not the world's most exciting read, however, and it can be confusing until you realise that you are given the same information three times in different forms.

The information also has to be taken with a small or large pinch of salt, depending on your school's circumstances. Factors such as the size of the year group(s) reported on and their mobility can distort the results. If the year group is smaller than roughly 25, as in the case of the Autumn Package the statistics are not particularly reliable, as under- or over-performance by just two pupils will have a marked effect on the figures. If a significant proportion of the year group has changed during the previous year, actual results can vary considerably from the targets, and if a large number have changed over the Key Stage, Key Stage comparisons are less valid. So if you are given reasons for apparently disappointing figures, these may be valid explanations, not excuses.

SATs and GCSE results

Long before you get the Autumn Package you will see the current year's SATs and GCSE results, which you are obliged to publish in your annual report to parents. They are commonly referred to as "raw" data, which means that they have not been analysed or interpreted in any way.

Any one year's results can be misleading when taken at face value. Each year group is different; each child is different. We need to know a lot more to make sense of the results:

- How many pupils/students took the tests?
- What proportion of the year group was absent?
- What was the ratio of boys to girls in the group?
- How many of the pupils left or joined the school during the period leading up to the test?
- How did each pupil's results compare with their previous test results?
- Were there any significant staff changes during the Key Stage?

There will be more factors that need consideration in your school's context, but these will do as a starter. The information contained in the Autumn Package will enable you to analyse and interpret your school's results properly – though there's an inevitable and frustrating time gap between the publication of the results and the Autumn Package. Many schools get on with the analysis long before the package comes out.

LEA adviser reports

It is very common for each school in an LEA to be allocated an adviser/inspector, whose job is to support and challenge the school. The adviser will probably visit at least once per year but might do so each term or more frequently. Often their work will be supplemented by a "desk top review" of the collected data on the school. As a result of the visit, the adviser will normally write a report. *Governance Matters* (COGS/TEN, 2002), a report written by Simon Bird of The Education Network, highlighted an unsatisfactory inconsistency of practice between LEAs in relation to the extent to which this information was shared with the governing body: "The high proportion of authorities who do not share their advisers' school monitoring reports with governors ... is a practice which is incompatible with governing bodies' statutory duty to promote high standards of education ... It is untenable to continue to deny governors access to these monitoring reports."

Clearly this is a controversial issue. You may be lucky and be a governor in a school in which this information is shared freely. If not, at least you know that the reports exist and could raise the question of your access to them.

The reports have the virtue of objectivity and frequency. They may well comment on specific areas of concern and/or improvement in the school. They should pose few problems in terms of interpretation, and they are written in straightforward language and to record observations and make recommendations.

Heads may argue that the reports are variable according to the quality and knowledge of the individual adviser/inspector and, therefore, less reliable than Ofsted reports. However, nearly all LEA adviser/inspectors are also Ofsted trained. Occasionally the report might "soft pedal", especially if the adviser/inspector has earnings targets to meet from continued work with the school and/or the relationship with the head is a little too cosy.

If these are matters of genuine concern, they need to be addressed through the LEA and the heads' associations. Otherwise, there is no reason for governors not to see the reports.

School-generated data

If the school is regularly collecting and using pupil-specific data to inform its work and improve pupil performance, then the quality of that data is likely to be as good as, if not better than, that contained in the PANDA report.

Some of the data will be "raw", including information on the number of pupil absences and exclusions. More useful is value-added data. This takes account of a pupil's starting point as well as the final result achieved, compared to national standards and pupils in similar schools. Some schools do this analysis themselves but many use commercially published resources and/or software packages in order to save time and achieve a professional looking analysis. Value-added analyses enable you to identify the extent to which pupils, teachers and the school in general have exceeded expectations – or not, as the case may be.

We don't necessarily need to see all the school-generated data, just to know that it's being used in teachers' planning and pupil target-setting. But we do need to know what measures the school is taking to address any issues raised by the analysis, such as offsetting the worst effects of a shifting school population if that's a feature of the school.

One of the key documents in which you will (or should be able to) find school-generated information on pupil performance is the headteacher's report to the governing body, as discussed at the end of chapter 2.

READING THE DATA

Who deals with the data?

Some of the data is intended for governors, some not. For example, the PANDA is written for an audience that includes governors, although they are unlikely to receive an individual copy each – and that isn't necessary, anyway. On the other hand, if a committee is responsible for monitoring and evaluation data, it would not be unreasonable for each member to have a copy of the relevant information.

Often the head will have done the analysis before the governors have had a chance to examine the data. They will be presented with an analysis which can then form the basis of a discussion which is essentially evaluative. This practice would seem to be in line with the DfES and Ofsted advice given earlier in the chapter. This might happen at the level of a full governing body meeting, which is ideal, although you'll need to allow plenty of time for this item – possibly a single item agenda.

In other situations, a single governor or a committee might be the instigator of the discussion. Sometimes the best data analyst in the school is a member of the governing body! Not all heads are confident in their interpretation and use of data. Some may prefer not to share the data for fear of exposing this weakness. Others may feel protective of the governors, not wanting to shower them with yet more paperwork. Very occasionally, a head may try to hide the information for a variety of possible reasons.

What if the head doesn't share the data with us?

Now you know what you're entitled to see, what do you do if the head is not passing on the right information? You want the information but you probably don't want to run the risk of alienating him/her, so proceed with caution.

Try to work out why the head is behaving in this way. Is it a cock-up or a conspiracy? Is it insecurity? Is there a problem of confidentiality, real or perceived? Is one of the governors over-zealous in challenging the school and the head? Is the head a poor leader or manager? Is other information not being shared?

Check your perceptions with other governors. Each situation is unique, so there's never an off-the-peg solution. Once you've done your best to work out why the data isn't being shared, you could try one or more of the following strategies:

- Ask the chair to ask the head for the data.
- Ask an appropriate committee chair to request the data.
- Talk to the head about it, if you've tried the first two approaches and they have failed.

If the data is still not forthcoming, it has become a serious issue and the chair should take responsibility on behalf of the governing body. The chair could download the relevant data from the appropriate website and/or approach the school's LEA adviser to see if he/she could help to improve the flow of information.

It's unlikely that things will need to be taken this far but, ultimately, governors are responsible for ensuring that standards are as high as they could be and they can only be assured of that by seeing the hard data for themselves. Ofsted, the DfES and the LEA all expect heads to share such data with governors. In the previous version of the National Standards for Headteachers (under revision at the time of writing), which form the basis for all headteachers' national qualifications, you'll find the following:

Headteachers provide information, objective advice and support to the governing body to enable it to meet its responsibilities for securing effective teaching and learning and improved standards of achievement, and for achieving efficiency and value for money.

So there's no excuse for a head not to share information with governors!

We all need to know

It may well be that on your governing body the analysis and evaluation of performance data is left to an individual or, more commonly, a committee, such as the Curriculum Committee. There is nothing inherently wrong with this but there is a danger that the full governing body may not be as well informed as it should be. Some governors might welcome this, particularly those for whom statistics is a closed book. But Ofsted expects all governors to know the strengths and weaknesses of the school – and the evidence upon which that analysis is based. So, one way or another, all members of the governing body need to know what the PANDA report says – in terms of key messages rather than fine detail, how valid it is, what other data is available to complement the PANDA and what the school intends to do in order to address the areas for improvement identified by analysis. Monitoring and evaluating performance data leads to target setting. In the case of KS2 and 4, setting the targets by the end of December for the next year's cohort provides the impetus for the school to analyse data in the autumn term.

So, we know something about what data should be available to us and that we're meant to evaluate it by asking challenging questions. This is part of school accountability – we have a statutory duty to ensure that the school is providing the best possible education for all its pupils.

That's fine, as long as we take the view that the statistical data is all that we need to make that judgement. But statistics are notoriously fallible and pliable – even statisticians tell the joke of the statistician who drowned in a river, having reckoned it was safe to walk through because the average depth was three feet. If you torture statistics long enough, they'll confess to anything. And there's more to education than a limited range of results.

4. THE CURRICULUM, PLANS AND POLICIES

The three areas for monitoring and evaluation that *Making It Better* recommends are the action plan, school improvement plan and the curriculum. The first two are relatively easy. The third is, frankly, impossible – and unnecessary, if the head is leading and managing the school properly.

THE CURRICULUM

It's easy to fall into the trap of thinking that the curriculum is just the National Curriculum – all eleven subjects, including Citizenship – since the sheer overload of subjects can't be covered fully in any school week. It doesn't leave space for anything else. But children learn all the time – out of school as well as in. In school, every aspect of learning constitutes part of the curriculum, whether it's intended or not. Naturally, it would be impossible for any teacher to monitor every single learning experience of every child in their class, so there's absolutely no chance of a governor being able to do it.

This is not to say, though, that we should simply abandon our responsibility to ensure high standards and common access to a broad, balanced curriculum. We need to work out which vital elements we can monitor and evaluate successfully. How might we do that?

This is Ofsted's advice:

> Governors should monitor the curriculum in different ways. First, they need to check that the school's curriculum is meeting national requirements, and that all subjects taught have a scheme of work.

Making It Better, Ofsted, 2001

The second way of monitoring the curriculum, according to *Making It Better*, is through analysing performance data, as we saw in the previous chapter. That is an achievable and worthwhile task – though it's more to do with evaluation than monitoring.

To return to the first suggestion, though, how would you know whether or not your school's curriculum was meeting national requirements? What are national requirements, anyway? Would you be aware if they'd changed in the last year or so? Policing this directly would be a huge task.

If you really wanted to – though I wouldn't recommend it, and you probably haven't the time to do it – you *could* start with the National Curriculum itself, which is a reasonably readable though substantial document. You'd need to absorb and be able to recall significant chunks of detail. You could then ask to see Schemes of Work for all subjects and match them against National Curriculum requirements. You'd also need to be aware of the detail of more recent initiatives such as the literacy and numeracy strands of the National Primary Strategy and the Key Stage 3 Strategy in secondary schools.

Then you'd have to find out if all the teachers were, to use an awful DfES word, "delivering" the curriculum. At its most extreme, this would take daily monitoring in classrooms against the Schemes of Work.

There's no point in our trying to do it, since it's what teachers and other staff are doing day in, day out.

What curriculum monitoring entails

> There are schools where governance is judged to be good but leadership and management are unsatisfactory. These schools are characterised by having a governing body that is fully involved in monitoring all aspects of the school and taking a deep interest in their work. These governing bodies generally have a clear understanding of the school's strengths and weaknesses and are, therefore, influential in giving the school a very clear direction.
>
> *The Work of School Governors,* Ofsted 2002

This telling quotation suggests that "monitoring all aspects of the school" is really only necessary by default, in a school in which the leadership team is not doing its job.

Remember the DfES's guidance:

> Governing bodies will need to monitor progress, but are not responsible for collecting monitoring data themselves.

One of the headteacher's key tasks is to ensure that the curriculum is being taught properly and in accordance with statutory requirements. We must rely on the head to give us the monitoring information we need to discharge our responsibilities. Our role – again – must be to monitor the monitoring. We need to know that the head (directly or via appropriate delegation) ensures that:

- teachers' planning is thorough and relevant
- teaching and learning are as effective as possible
- statutory curriculum requirements are met.

We can certainly experience these things at first hand in order to complement our evaluation of performance data and deepen our understanding of the school, but it's not our job to do the first-hand monitoring. Our job is to ensure that we get from the head, primarily, the evidence and information we need in order to evaluate how well the curriculum is being led, managed and taught. If statutory requirements are not being met, the head should tell us via their report to the governing body or we will know from our last Ofsted inspection report, or, in some cases, from the LEA adviser's report. These might have come too late for one or two governing bodies who have been misled, but for the vast majority, it's unlikely to be a major concern.

There are practical ways in which governors can experience the curriculum directly and these are discussed in chapter 6.

PLANS

Plans both derive from and work towards achieving an exciting, imaginative vision of the school in the future. Ideally, we should have a current, detailed one-year operational plan and a mid-term strategic plan. If we've been inspected recently, we'll be working on a post-inspection action plan which will need to merge with our school improvement (or development) plan.

If the plans are properly thought out, our monitoring and evaluation should be straightforward, though much depends on the quality and precision of the success criteria. It's still common to come across success criteria which are merely the extension of the action plan. For example, the action might be "To produce a new Scheme of Work for History" and the success criterion "New Scheme of Work produced". This doesn't get us very far. This shows clearly the practical distinction between monitoring and evaluation – the criterion given is fine for monitoring purposes, but does not get you anywhere with evaluation.

A good success criterion will define the impact of the action in terms of measurable outcomes or benefits for children, in the main. The impetus for producing a new Scheme of Work for History might be the need to fulfil statutory requirements but we must ask ourselves "How will it improve things for the pupils or students?" It should, for example, ensure that the needs of all learners are catered for, so one outcome might be that the test results in History for pupils with Special Educational Needs increase by x percent. As a general rule, beginning the criteria with the stem: "Pupils will..." or "Students will..." tends to focus attention on the most important outcomes and, as stated in the remark above, make you evaluate.

There is a danger, however, that we try to find a success criterion for every single action in the plan, which is not usually necessary or helpful. Instead we might group together linked actions

---

Plan pro forma – Primary school example

OVERALL OBJECTIVE: Increase the rate of progress of all pupils, including girls and higher attaining pupils, in reading, writing and science

SUCCESS CRITERION: By (specific date) all pupils irrespective of gender or ability to make progress that matches or exceeds the progress of pupils nationally in reading, writing and science at KS2.

TARGET 2 **Improve attainment in writing**

MONITORING AND EVALUATION:
LEAD PERSON: Headteacher   OTHERS INVOLVED: Literacy Adviser, Chair of Governors, Literacy Governor

Action	Start Date	End Date	Staff Time	Support Needed	Cost
2.1 Seek advice from the LEA Adviser to audit present work and practice	4/10/04	29/11/04		Literacy Adviser – 1 day?	£240
2.2 Review whole school Scheme of Work for writing	4/10/04	7/1/05	Staff mtg. Teacher Dev'ment day		
2.3 Arrange for teachers to visit other schools to observe good practice in literacy	4/10/04	3/4/05	5 days' supply		£600
2.4 Review criteria for moderating children's writing and ensure consistency of judgements	4/10/04	29/11/04	Staff meetings		
2.5 Set termly assessment tasks and track children's progress	4/10/04	ongoing			

Plan pro forma – Secondary school example		
Objective	**Actions**	**Success criterion**
Improve the attitudes and behaviour of pupils in Key Stage 3	Enhance induction programme for new Year 7 students 1. Identify excluded students from primary schools early and implement pre-emptive strategies, e.g. involvement of parents. 2. Produce induction video for all Year 6 students on the subject of expectations. 3. Bring Year 7 into school on first day of term with sixth form only. 4. Timetable PSHE & Citizenship to ensure circle time work takes place. 5. Run Year 7 team-building day early in Autumn Term.	**By July 2005** 10% reduction in fixed-term exclusions *cf.* previous year

for a range of subjects (such as Humanities), with one or two key success criteria whereby all will be evaluated.

The success criteria should help us to identify what evidence we will need to collect through the monitoring process in order to evaluate the success or otherwise of a particular action or set of actions.

In the examples the actions would be monitored by the members of staff responsible for making sure they happened. Each action will have a timescale and a named monitor (omitted from the secondary example, for brevity). It would be interesting to know not just that the action had taken place, which is all that the process of monitoring is meant to do, at its most basic, but also what impact each action had had. This, again, is a matter of monitoring versus evaluation.

For example, we will want to be assured that in the secondary school example the induction video for Year 6 was not only made (monitoring) and used but also that it ensured that those children coming to our school had a clearer set of expectations than would otherwise have been the case (evaluation). How could this be measured? Staff might interview a sample of the previous year's intake about the clarity of their expectations, as they remembered them and where their ideas of what was expected had come from. This could be compared to a survey of Year 6 pupils before watching the video, then again after a few weeks at the new school. Such anecdotal evidence is probably the closest you'll get to knowing whether what took place had any real effect.

It takes time and forethought to do this kind of assessment properly, and teachers may well argue that they don't have the time to do it. When the improvement plan is being assembled, consideration should be given to what evidence of impact will be needed when we come to the evaluation stage. At the same time, a realistic estimate of how much time such evidence collection will take, and who will do it and when, need to be built in to the plan. If this is done properly, it may become apparent that there really isn't sufficient capacity to evaluate as fully as we intended, in which case there is no choice but to scale down the process.

Assessing impact is evaluation. The success criterion is a way of measuring the combined effect of all the actions at the end of a specified period of time.

Time is of the essence

Time scales are very important. Successful monitoring depends on establishing *several* key dates or milestones to help us judge progress in any one action – though how many depends on the complexity of the action plan. If we ascribe a completion date as "summer term", we're as good as saying "We're not too serious about carrying out this action". If, however, we write "10th July" – and we write it in our diaries – the chances are much higher that we will actually make sure it happens. The same logic applies to when we intend to evaluate the impact of an aspect of the action plan: "10th July, 11 am, Head's office" says "We really mean to do this."

It is common in education that by the time we get round to thinking about evaluating the last plan, we've already written and are working on the new one. This is partly the result of the pace of life in schools and, sometimes, if we're honest, a reluctance to face the difficult question "What difference did it make?" that lies at the heart of evaluation. What if the answer is "not much" or "none at all"? And what if we've rolled forward some or all of that plan into the new one?

Evaluation day

Finding the time to evaluate the curriculum and the school improvement plan presents most governors with a real problem. One very practical solution to this dilemma is to set aside an evaluation day each year, timed to inform the construction of the new school improvement plan. It may mean that not every part of the plan is yet complete but we should have sufficient evidence to make some key judgements. The evaluators on the day could include governors, headteacher, senior staff, teachers, support staff, pupils/students and the school's LEA adviser. One possible scheme for the day is at various times to:

- look at some of the key performance data
- hear from some teachers about particular projects they've been working on
- look at examples of children's work and hear from them about what they've achieved
- hear how the governors have been involved in school improvement.

In an ideal world, we would follow up this day with another where we work together on the new plan, using the knowledge gained from the review to inform our thinking.

POLICIES

As of spring 2004 the following policies are a legal requirement:

- Admissions (foundation and voluntary aided schools)
- Careers education and information (secondary schools)
- Charging
- Child protection
- Complaints
- Complaints against the curriculum
- Curriculum
- Health & Safety
- Home-school agreements
- Lettings

- Nutritional standards
- Performance management
- Pupil discipline
- Race equality
- Registration of pupils
- School session times
- Schemes for paying governors' allowances
- Sex education
- Special Educational Needs
- Staff discipline - rules on grievance procedure
- Target-setting.

In addition, schools and governing bodies may well have a pile of other policies of their own.

Let's assume you have the required policies in place. As with the school improvement plan, you might have included in each policy at the time it was written or last reviewed some indication of how it would be monitored and evaluated, who would be responsible and how it would be done. If you've done so, provided everyone does what they are supposed to do, there should not be a problem.

A policy framework

A useful structure for any policy is offered in Michele Robbins' and Martin Baxter's *Policies: A guide for school governors and headteachers* (Adamson Books, 2003):

- Purpose (link to school vision and values)
- Who/what was consulted - staff/pupils/parents/LEA/Diocese/others/guidance documentation?
- Relationship to other school policies
- Roles and responsibilities of head, other staff, governors
- Arrangements for monitoring and evaluation
- Date established by governing body
- Date for review.

By and large we're more likely to be concerned with reviewing (or evaluating) each policy than with the day-to-day monitoring, which is likely to be the preserve of those working in the school. Remember that Ofsted's S3 form is a very effective way of ensuring that all key statutory responsibilities are met – in most cases by having an up-to-date policy in place – and implemented.

We can make excellent use of our committees to review policies by allocating relevant policies to each committee. The review dates included in each policy can be sequenced against the committees' meetings schedule to ensure all are reviewed at the appropriate time. Of course, different policies will need to be reviewed at differing frequencies. Some may merit an annual review, others may only need looking at every three years, say.

Our review should look at how workable the policy is and whether it is still up to date in light of recent legislation or regulations. The key evaluation question is, predictably, "What difference has the policy made?"

5. THE BUDGET

Governors are formally required to agree the school's spending plan (i.e. the budget) and monitor the way the money is spent through the year. The governing body must also apply the principles of Best Value (explained later in this chapter) to their spending decisions, which, in effect, means evaluating the budget. Much of the detailed work will be done by the finance committee, but it should be done in the context of the overall needs of the school. The budget should be driven by the school's improvement plan and day-to-day needs rather than the budget driving the school.

MONITORING

Many governors' eyes glaze over when faced with pages of figures and budget headings. For those not on the finance committee it's tempting to leave it all to them and the other people involved in school finance, such as the head, the bursar or administrative officer and the LEA's support accountants. But you have a collective responsibility to monitor the budget, so it can't be avoided – and in extreme cases it could even prove dangerous to entrust large sums of public money to a small group of people in the know. The monitoring process enables you to track the progress of your collective decisions on spending and should help you to evaluate the impact of your strategic decisions at the end of the financial year.

The good news is that you don't have to be a financial expert to get on top of school budgets. The principles are the same as for your domestic budget. As with the domestic costs you have to pay like mortgage, phone, electricity and community charge, most of your school's income is accounted for before you get it, going on salaries, water, heating, lighting, furniture, cleaning and so on. The sum we're left with to manage creatively can be as little as 1 percent of the budget. However, sometimes you need to take a close, hard look at standing spending commitments, and this can save significant sums, especially where sums are increased annually on the basis of historical spending. More of the same is not always the best policy. Investing now to save in the longer term can be a better option.

A good example of this is the DfES's "Remodelling the Workforce" policy, which challenges us to review how we deploy our staff and make the best possible use of the professional skills they have. Relying on teachers' goodwill to cover basic administrative tasks is no longer an option. We need to professionalise school administration, and while this may seem expensive initially, in the longer term it should save money and establish a more effective and efficient system. For example, employing a professional school librarian can mean an increase in library use, better maintenance of book stock, more effective library management systems and the release of the time of whoever was struggling to do the job previously!

As a member of the governing body – if not a member of the finance committee – you should see regular budget monitoring information through the year. This might be monthly but is more likely to be termly, as part of the agenda of your governing body meetings. The information will probably have been prepared by the finance committee, who will have done the detailed checking. Much will depend on how it's presented. Computer printouts from standard school finance software, such as SIMS, are notoriously difficult to interpret, even by those who are used to them. If you're lucky, someone will have taken the trouble to simplify the information by grouping together many individual budget lines under broad headings, such as salaries, services and so on. You really only need to see the fine detail if you think there could be a problem somewhere.

If you don't understand the information you're given, don't be afraid to say so. The chances are that others round the table may well breathe a deep sigh of relief that someone's voiced their own problems. Those who prepare the information may not have understood why others may not grasp it as quickly as they do.

Ideally, you'll receive a form that includes the following:

- a column of broad budget lines or headings (salaries, furniture and fittings, etc.)
- a column showing how much you allocated to each budget heading when you originally set the budget
- a column showing the amount you expected to have spent by now on each area of spending (called the forecast or profiled expenditure)
- a column showing the amount you have actually spent
- a column showing the difference between the sums in the previous two columns (i.e. what you thought you would have spent and what you've actually spent).

Here's a *very* simplified example. Let's imagine you receive this extract from a budget statement in September. In reality, of course, it would be longer and more detailed, covering all areas of income and expenditure.

Category	Annual Budget	Forecast Expenditure (A)	Actual Expenditure (B)	Variance (B − A)
Salaries: teaching	171637	85099	85027	−72
Salaries: admin/clerical	7975	3961	3948	−13
Supply teachers	2835	1292	2954	1662
Water	1796	898	1477	579
Gas	6301	2005	1997	−8
Electricity	2839	949	1006	57
TOTALS	193383	94204	96409	2205

A minus figure represents an underspend. This is the good news! The bad news is that what at first glance might appear to be a healthy balance at the end of the sheet is, in fact, an overspend.

This statement represents the situation half way through the financial year. What has been happening in the school?

Evidence	Likely cause	Action/Remedy
Expenditure on supply staff is higher than the forecast.	Staff absence – one or more teachers ill	Find out details of staff absence; how many staff? How long?
Expenditure on water is greater than anticipated.	Water leak	Find and repair leak
The final balance shows the school heading for an overspend.	See above	Use underspent categories to offset overspend.

What should we be looking at?

If the above is the first monitoring statement you've seen this year, then there's a problem. Regular, understandable reports are essential if you are to stand a chance of doing the job properly. You should have a report for each meeting of the full governing body, at the very least.

Staff absence

Did you get your predictions right? Predicting how much you'll need to spend on supply teachers is one of the hardest aspects of budget planning and monitoring. You may have a couple of years in which there's very little staff absence, so you get lulled into a false sense of security and then get hit by a flu epidemic the next year, wiping out your provision and more. Analysing staff absence rates over, say, five years can help establish an average. You can take out insurance against staff absence, though it can prove expensive. The shorter the period of absence before the policy kicks in, the costlier it is.

Staff absence could be a reflection of poor management. If there are wild fluctuations from year to year, you could find out if there are any common explanatory factors and then plan to address them. Are some staff regularly absent on a particular day? Does staff absence increase in proportion to the length of the school term? Is there a culture of overwork created through the head's very long hours?

Water leak

The effects of a small water leak may not be noticed for a few months. Only careful regular monitoring will show it up for what it is – and you'll have to spend to get it repaired, in order to save in the longer term. You don't have a choice, though you may have to wait a while before you can afford to fix it.

The overspend

You must start moving (or "viring") money from underspent areas to those where you're currently overspending. You may be lucky and find that you have sufficient unspent money to balance the books. However, in so doing you will have harmed your ability to deliver on all the priorities you originally set, so these will also have to be reviewed and revised.

You might be tempted to try fundraising. At present fundraising is one of the few responsibilities governors don't have – at least in a statutory sense. But the reality is that governors often do get involved.

You might find that, having reviewed and revised as much as you possibly can, you still can't balance the books. In this case you will need to approach the LEA to agree a repayment of the overspend, usually over a 3 to 5 year period. This is known as a deficit budget.

The worst scenario is where the LEA comes to the conclusion that the governing body is incapable of managing the budget effectively and "withdraws delegation". This means that LEA officers take over running the budget for a given period of time until things are back on track.

EVALUATION

How do you know if your spending is as cost-effective as possible? To find out, you apply the principles of Best Value. The DfES outlines these in guidance:

> Best Value goes beyond the value for money principles of economy, efficiency and effectiveness, which successful school managers have long applied. Value for money does lie at the core of Best Value. However, Best Value develops it into the idea that close partnership with those served by the school and the effective use of resources leads to:
>
> • the raising of education standards; and
>
> • continuous improvement.
>
> Best Value should not be seen as a new process, rather an opportunity to improve the ways in which management decisions are made. It should infuse the overall approach to school management and evaluation. Best Value can help schools to improve performance by applying its principles. The principles of Best Value are known familiarly as the Four Cs:
>
> • Challenge – why, how and by whom an activity is carried out
>
> • Compare – performance against other schools and between parts of each school
>
> • Consult – involving stakeholders, especially pupils and parents, and
>
> • Compete – as a means of securing efficient and effective services.
>
> The Four Cs can be considered separately for the sake of clarity. However, as schools make decisions, the principles are often applied in combination."

Best Value in Schools, DfES, 2000

Using the principles of Best Value

The last-but-one edition of the *Handbook for Inspecting Nursery and Primary Schools* (Ofsted, 2000) provided an excellent summary of working with Best Value and showed the kinds of questions governors need to ask in assessing to what extent their school provides it:

> The Best Value approach does not apply statutorily to governing bodies in their use of delegated and devolved budgets. However, governing bodies are required to set targets to raise standards, are expected to provide a good-quality public service, and spend public money wisely. Schools are accountable for balancing *costs* (in terms of economy and efficiency) and *effectiveness* (in terms of their performance and the quality of what they provide) as required by the Best Value framework. To achieve this schools need to demonstrate that they apply Best Value principles in arriving at decisions about all their activities, especially how the financial resources delegated to them are managed.

Compare

Comparison of performance against that of all schools and similar schools is readily possible for schools. PANDA reports and other data provide suitable benchmarks and other indicators to enable the school to monitor its performance, measure it against others and set targets. Find out the extent to which the school asks itself, and answers, such questions as:

- What is the quality of education provided by similar schools?

- How do our standards compare with theirs?

- Are we a relatively high performer?

- Do we cost more or less than others?

- Why?

Challenge
This is about whether the school challenges itself about the services it provides. Does the school take steps, for example, to find out whether what it provides is what is needed, within the discretion allowed in the statutory framework for the curriculum and outside the statutory minimum? Although, for primary schools, the National Curriculum is not negotiable, other aspects of provision are. Does the introduction of primary French, a "silent reading" period for every class, or a part-time play group on the school premises, for example, fulfil the conditions of Best Value? Find out the extent to which the school asks itself such questions as:

- Why are we doing this?

- Is it what people want?

- What is the evidence about level of need?

- Could someone else do it differently, or better?

Consult
This is about being clear what the school community wants. When considering major changes or spending decisions, involving the curriculum provided or other major developments, does the school seek the views of those most concerned, and how does it respond to those views? This means asking or getting feedback from staff, parents, pupils and others on:

- what they want the school to do;

- what they think of proposed changes or major expenditure;

- whether they are happy with, or at, the school;

- what is in their best interests.

Did the school consult parents, for example, when drawing up a post-inspection action plan? or when changing the balance of the curriculum? Or does it just announce such matters? Increasingly, schools use questionnaires to survey parents; many also periodically seek the views of pupils. Some schools have a pupils' council. Indeed some involve pupils to the extent of producing a version of the summary inspection report specially written for pupils.

Compete

Competition is concerned both with whether the school is doing anything which could be better provided by someone else, and with the strategic use of resources and getting best value for expenditure. Does the school have proper financial administration procedures, including competitive tendering for significant expenditure? Examples might include supply and part-time staff, in-service training, expenditure on equipment and maintenance contracts. Is purchasing on a fair and open basis or through personal connection, or is one supplier used regardless of price? The school should be asking questions like:

- Are we providing the service at the right price?

- Could we or others provide it at a better price?

- What do the users of this service want?

- What is in the best interest of pupils and parents?

- How does the school ensure it receives the most economic, efficient and effective service from those who provide services to pupils and staff?

Clearly, working through the four Cs means that you cover some of the same territory that we explored earlier, but ensures that you're not missing anything vital in your evaluation. Again, some or much of the monitoring evidence you need to inform your evaluative judgements will be supplied by the professionals in your school, so you shouldn't need to get involved in any direct monitoring yourselves.

Using the 4 Cs is a valuable activity, not least because the questions listed above demonstrate that finance is not a vacuum-packed isolated area of activity but is part and parcel of the whole school improvement process. Just getting the columns of figures to add up is not sufficient.

Further help

Further help is readily available from three publications from the Audit Commission.

Getting the Best from Your Budget is a guide to effective management in schools. It explores the decision-making processes that help schools to focus their resources on improvement. The booklet includes practical illustrations of how schools can successfully implement these principles. It can be downloaded from both http://www.ofsted.gov.uk/public/docs00/budget.pdf and http://www.audit-commission.gov.uk/publications/pdf/brbalanc.pdf.

Controlling School Finances is designed to help schools assess how far they comply with the standards set out in *Keeping Your Balance*. The website provides good practice guidance, and the system will generate a score to tell schools how well they are doing, together with a series of feedback tables and a prioritised action plan. It provides information on budget reviews and can help to guard against unhelpful historic spending patterns.

Keeping Your Balance is published jointly with Ofsted. It is a guide to financial management and provides a set of standards for financial management and control, taking account of the increased level of delegation and financial responsibility introduced in the School Standards and Framework Act 1998. Available on http://www.ofsted.gov.uk/public/docs00/balance.pdf and http://www.audit-commission.gov.uk/publications/brbalance.shtml.

Benchmarking expenditure is a way for schools to take control of their budgets by learning from others and implementing changes to spending patterns to help them deliver their education priorities. The Schools Financial Benchmarking database contains information about the income and expenditure of over 20,000 schools and provides school managers and governors with the tools to benchmark their finances and help them to manage finite resources effectively. You can find it on the TeacherNet website at www.teachernet.gov.uk/management/tools/schoolfinance. It enables you to prepare charts that compare your school's income and expenditure profile with that of similar schools. Any school, LEA or guest can use this part of the site and select its own group of similar schools, using a range of factors such as size, type, percentage with special needs and so on. A school or LEA user is required to log in using a username and password.

6. THE SCHOOL ENVIRONMENT

Monitoring and evaluation of the school environment by governors comes down to two essential activities and one optional one. The essential ones, on which you have to report to parents, are to do with security and accessibility. The optional – though highly desirable – activity is visiting the school. As we will see, though, the focus is not on monitoring or evaluating the teachers but the environment in which they teach and children learn.

SECURITY

Security is not quite the same thing as Health and Safety, although they are connected in some ways. One of the key elements of any Health and Safety policy is an annual risk assessment, which involves governors and others touring the school to identify potential hazards and then assessing the level of risk posed by any that are found. The really high risk factors will have to be put right, of course, but the rest can remain, so long as you ensure anyone using the school is aware of them.

While carrying out this inspection you should also be thinking about and looking for opportunities to improve school security. This does not necessarily imply installing high tech systems, such as CCTV, although some schools choose to do so. Often the most effective improvements in school security do not cost money – or, at worst, only small sums. They are usually to do with routines and behaviour, such as a visitors' log and badge system.

DfES guidance on security

The DfES's guidance on the content of annual reports includes the following examples of security matters:

- a summary of the school's security policy

- arrangements for reviewing security including the timing and frequency of reviews and details of any bodies from whom security advice has been or will be sought

- any action taken by the school, LEA, or trustees to improve the safety of pupils and staff and the security of the premises

- details of any recent significant incidents, e.g. assaults on staff or pupils, theft, vandalism or arson.

Information should not be provided which may increase the risk to the school, e.g. information which draws attention to specific security weaknesses or details of alarm systems.

High-profile tragedies, such as the shooting at Dunblane, have heightened schools' awareness of the need for security, but this has to be balanced with the desire to create and sustain an ethos of openness and a welcoming atmosphere.

Monitoring and evaluation of the school's security policy will fall to the members of the relevant governing body committee in most schools. This may well be a premises committee, whose remit will cover the school site and its buildings, health and safety, access and security issues. Their monitoring role will include noting the school's log of "significant incidents" as listed above. They will evaluate the effectiveness of the school's security arrangements by, for example, comparing the number and nature of incidents recorded in the log from one year to another, then deciding on any action for improvement that seems necessary.

ACCESSIBILITY

From September 2002 it became unlawful for governing bodies to discriminate against disabled pupils and prospective pupils in the provision of education and associated services in schools, and in admissions and exclusions. This means that schools have to be made accessible for all pupils, including those with disabilities. This does not just mean physical access to the buildings but includes access to all aspects of the curriculum.

All governing bodies should check that their school reviews its policies, practices and procedures on a continuing basis to ensure that disabled children will not be placed at a substantial disadvantage. Governing bodies are liable for acts of discrimination in their schools. If a claim of discrimination is made against a school, to defend itself the governing body will need to demonstrate that it had taken all reasonable steps to prevent that discrimination occurring.

In considering what steps are "reasonable", a school can take account of:

- the need to maintain academic and other standards
- the financial resources available
- the practicality of taking particular steps
- the health and safety of the disabled pupil or others in the school
- the interests of other pupils who may be admitted to the school, including issues of disruption.

Governing bodies will want to ensure that employees and others working in the school:

- *do not* act in such a way as to render the governing body liable to a claim for discrimination
- *do* receive appropriate guidance and support the governors in meeting their duties to pupils.

Defining disability

Helpful advice is provided in the DfES's guidance, which includes a definition of disability:

> A disabled person is one who has "a physical or mental impairment which has a substantial and long-term adverse effect on a person's ability to carry out normal day-to-day activities". This would include, for example, sensory impairments affecting sight and hearing, learning disabilities, severe disfigurements and progressive conditions where impairments are likely to become substantial.

It also describes the need for the school to prepare an accessibility plan setting out plans for increasing disability access to the school.

How to do it

By and large, the information you need will be provided by the head and the school's Special Educational Needs Co-ordinator (SENCO), so you don't need to monitor the practice yourselves, other than to be assured it's taking place. Members of the premises (or equivalent) committee should take responsibility for the details of existing facilities (the monitoring and evaluation of which could also be included in the risk assessment inspection) and for drawing up the accessibility plan, in conjunction with the head and SENCO. The plan should include details of arrangements for monitoring and evaluation, as with the other plans described earlier.

VISITING THE SCHOOL

School and (especially) classroom visits do not sit easily in the context of a book about governors' monitoring and evaluation, since it has been argued earlier that one of the governors' key tasks is to monitor the monitoring rather than actively engage in first-hand monitoring, which a classroom visit appears to suggest. *Classroom visiting is certainly not about monitoring the teachers in the school.*

Ofsted have sometimes given the impression that governors should monitor the school through regular visiting (e.g. in *Making It Better*). The main reason for discussing it here is to try to dispel that notion.

At its worst, classroom visiting implies the vision of an uninformed governor marching into a classroom, clipboard and checklist at the ready, prepared to make judgements about the teacher's professional skills, attitudes and behaviour. If that happened, it would be the kiss-of-death for any direct experience of the school for any governors for many years to come.

Public servants are under much more direct scrutiny than ever before and teachers have come to terms with Ofsted inspection and lesson observations by the head, LEA advisers and other teachers. Classrooms are far less secret than they used to be – but they are still the teachers' professional territory and a sensitive area. Some governors feel that the teaching profession is over-sensitive and defensive compared to the organisations from which they themselves come. That may be true but it doesn't help to build an effective partnership between teachers and governors if governors ignore any misgivings and simply barge in to inspect them.

The purpose of visits

Visits to the school and classroom are not a statutory requirement of the individual governor, but they can add immeasurably to the quality of understanding of the reality of school life. *The Guide to the Law for School Governors* (DfES, 2004) makes this abundantly clear:

> Individual governors do not have an automatic right to enter the school. But they do need to be able to visit from time to time in order to develop their understanding of how the school works to enable them to better fulfil their statutory responsibility for the conduct of the school.

> Governors should arrange their visits with the head, who has responsibility for the day-to-day management of the school. It is often useful to draw up a policy on governors visiting the school to cover things such as giving notice, constructive feedback and handling concerns. The governing body should plan visits to cover a wide range of school work and each visit should have a clear purpose.

> Visits by governors can be useful and informative. They do not replace professional inspection or the monitoring and evaluation carried out by the head teacher.

First and foremost, classroom visits are for the governor's own education, to see daily life in the classroom for the children, teachers and support staff. This should enhance the quality of discussions and decision-making by the governing body, avoiding the dangers of doing so in an abstract way, without any ability to envisage the impact of a policy decision on the classroom.

Visits make most sense in the context of a system of specific curriculum or class responsibilities for governors. Linking individual governors to curriculum areas, teachers, classes or year groups helps the governing body to understand something about the curriculum and teaching and learning. With this commonly used arrangement the governor can see for himself or herself how the teacher turns plans into practice in the classroom.

Why link governors to subjects or classes?

While governors do not need to be curriculum experts, they do need, collectively, a broad understanding of the curriculum. But, as we've seen, the curriculum is huge. It therefore makes sense to make the task manageable by encouraging each governor to learn more about one particular subject.

In addition to the main tasks given in the box below, the subject-link governor might consider including some or all of the following:

* receiving regular minutes and reports from their curriculum area
* attending a termly meeting with the curriculum area co-ordinator
* attending meetings involving development planning
* informing the co-ordinator of relevant outcomes of governing body meetings and providing clarification when necessary
* forming part of the interview panel for appointments in the curriculum area
* shadowing the co-ordinator, by arrangement and agreement.

The role of subject-/class-link governors
* to provide a link between the governing body and relevant teacher
* to provide a link between the governing body, the school and the parents and community
* to promote the interests of the subject
* to undertake relevant training/development
* to liaise regularly with relevant teachers
* to find out about local activity and develop networks with governors in neighbouring schools
* to visit classrooms to observe the subject being taught
* to monitor/evaluate the provision and use of relevant resources

---

When meeting the teacher with whom you are linked, it can be useful to have some questions at the ready, with some ideas of what kind of territory the answers might cover. The following table tries to provide this. It should be stressed, though, that the questions appear deceptively simple! In fact, you're unlikely to get beyond even one per meeting, so don't try to work your way through them all at the first go. It is also a good idea for the questions to be shared with the teaching staff generally, so that everything is transparent and open.

Questions for visits

Question	Possible features of answer	Notes of answer
Help me to understand how you plan your lessons: how do you get from the National Curriculum to deciding what Karen or Tom will be doing in Science today?	National Curriculum Key stage plan Scheme of Work Year plan/term plan/week plan/daily plan Individual plan	
How do you judge how well pupils are learning and making progress?	Questioning in lessons Marking Assessments, including tests SATs Target-setting and achieving Value-added data	
What learning resources are available to your pupils and how do they learn effectively?	ICT – access to computers Use of library Classroom library Use of basics like pens and pencils Good labelling Borrowed resources	
How do you cope with the needs of different pupils?	Boys *v.* girls Most able SEN English as an Additional Language Badly behaved Disabled	
How do you decide to seat children and arrange the classroom? Does it ever vary and why?	Ability groups Mixed or single age groups Boy-girl patterns Different for different activities	
How do you encourage parents to be involved in their children's learning?	Regular contact Reports Parent evenings Letters Diaries	

Developing an effective classroom visits policy

If not carefully planned and agreed, classroom visits by governors can lead to mutual suspicion and awkwardness between governors and teachers. Done well, they can add enormously to governors' understanding of their school, its teachers and its pupils. A brief policy on classroom visits negotiated between the governing body and teaching staff is an essential first step before any visits take place.

The following guidance on drafting a policy, drawing on ideas from governors, heads and teachers, may be helpful. An *aide memoire* for individual governors and sample governor's visit report sheets are also included to help promote discussion when considering the issues involved.

POLICY ON VISITS

Successful, open negotiation is the key to developing effective policy and practice. There is no point in simply adopting a sample policy as it stands, as what works in one school will not work in another. Ideally, set aside two hours to complete the negotiation.

Various elements should be considered:

- purposes
- what it's not about
- protocols or ground rules
- how to feed back after the visit
- minimum commitment
- annual programme
- monitoring and review.

Purposes

What are the potential benefits to governors and teachers?

Governors and teachers should each draw up a list and then compare it to the other group's list. Look for and note the common ground that is likely to emerge. You may get something like the following table.

Purposes of visits	
POTENTIAL BENEFITS TO GOVERNOR	POTENTIAL BENEFITS TO TEACHERS
To recognise and celebrate success	To ensure governors understand the reality of the classroom
To develop relationships with the staff	
To get to know the children	To get to know the governors
To recognise different teaching styles	To understand better the governors' roles and responsibilities
To understand the environment in which teachers teach	To have an opportunity to reflect on practicethrough discussion
To see policies and schemes of work in action	To highlight the need for particular resources
To inform decision-making	
To find out what resources are needed and prioritise them	

You might also consider the benefits to pupils.

What it's not about

The crucial point to note here is that, as stated earlier, governors' visits to classrooms are *not a form of inspection* to make judgements about the professional expertise of the teacher. That remains a task for the head and/or other education professionals. It's easy enough to write this as a straightforward statement but real life is never that simple. For example, when we are invited to a new colleague's or friend's house for the first time, we are likely to find ourselves thinking "Oh, no! Those curtains with that carpet – ugh!" or "I love that table – I wonder how much they paid for it?" The crucial point is that we normally keep those judgements to ourselves, as we know that voicing them would be rude. We also know that our judgements are personal and a matter of individual taste. We might instead venture compliments, such as "Your garden's looking lovely at this time of year," or we might seek information: "Where did you find that gorgeous table?"

We cannot help but make judgements all the time, but it's what we do with them that matters – and accepting that our opinions are not necessarily well-informed.

Governors' visits are not for pursuing personal concerns, either, and especially not for wanting to check up on your own child.

So when we consider "What is classroom visiting not about?" the answers usually include the following:

- making judgements about the quality of teaching
- checking on the progress of own children
- pursuing personal agendas
- monopolising teachers' time.

Protocols or ground rules

One effective approach to defining and agreeing protocols or ground rules for visits involves considering what should always happen and what should never happen before, during and after a visit. You can produce a pro-forma to list these, either on a flipchart or printed sheet.

Here are some of the elements that might be included:

Visit protocols

	Always	Never
Before	arrange details of visit	turn up unannounced
	agree level of confidentiality	
	agree purpose of visit	
	discuss the context of the lesson to be observed	
During	observe any class guidelines/rules	walk in with a clipboard
	fulfil agreed purpose	
After	thank the teacher and the pupils	leave without a word
	discuss observations with teacher	

Appropriate focuses for classroom visits might include:

- observation of one group of pupils working together on a task
- noting the relative numbers of questions and responses to the teacher from boys and girls
- observation of the Literacy Hour and/or Numeracy Hour.

It might also be worth discussing some "What ifs...?" to agree good practice. For example:

- What if I see children misbehaving when the teacher doesn't?
- What if a pupil asks me how to do something?
- What if the teacher has problems controlling the class?

The answer to these questions will vary from one school to another, which is why they need to be explored in each case. As *general* guidance, however, the following answers may help:

- *What if I see children misbehaving when the teacher doesn't?*
  It depends how serious the misbehaviour is and how frequently it happens. The occasional incident should probably be overlooked, but if the teacher is consistently failing to notice misbehaviour, it's something which should be taken up after the lesson. You could ask the teacher if they noticed a particular incident, for example, and what they would have done about it had it been noticed, or whether they chose to ignore it. If you still have major concerns, you may need to talk to the headteacher about it, in confidence. The head should find a way of following it up without suggesting in any way that you have reported a concern.

- *What if a pupil asks me how to do something?*
  It depends what it is. If it's something the teacher has already explained in the lesson, you can reinforce the teacher's message by explaining it again to the pupil. Otherwise, unless it's a trivial thing, you should ask the teacher on the pupil's behalf or encourage the pupil to ask the teacher directly. You might also be able to ask a teaching assistant, if one is present.

- *What if the teacher has problems controlling the class?*
  As with the first question, it depends on the level of poor control. Maintaining perfect class control at all times is not easy, especially in practical activities, so some leeway should be given. Also, a certain level of noise might just be a sign of enthusiastic participation in an activity. By and large, if a teacher is really struggling, the head would know about it anyway and not encourage a governor to visit in the first place. There will probably be some kind of support available for the teacher, possibly from a more senior colleague. But if control is obviously seriously lacking, then the head needs to be told.

Feedback

Consider:

To *whom* should governors feed back? Teacher? Headteacher? Head of department/faculty or subject/Key Stage co-ordinator? Governing body? Curriculum committee?

How should governors feed back? Verbally? In writing? With the teacher alongside?

What should they feed back? Positive comments? Areas of concern? Questions? Suggestions?

Feedback is perhaps the most difficult area to negotiate. On the one hand, the teacher won't appreciate you disappearing without saying anything, even if it's just "thanks for letting me sit in on the lesson". On the other, as soon as anything is written down, it becomes more "official". If it's to be given to other people, it might look like inspection. What you agree to do in your school, in close agreement with the teachers, is up to you. The least perilous approach is to agree simply to have a short chat with the teacher at the end of the lesson – and no more. If a focus has been agreed in advance, it provides the basis for a conversation.

However, if one of the agreed purposes of visiting is to develop a collective understanding of the school, then some kind of feedback to the governing body as a whole is necessary. The crucial thing to remember is that the report should not contain any comments on individual teachers. There are two sample feedback forms at the end of this section to illustrate what might be fed back and how.

If we decide to go further than this, we need to answer all the questions above, about who, what and how and agree our policy with the teachers and head. One way of overcoming any misgivings about how any reporting of the visit might be done is to ensure that the governor and teacher present it together at the committee or governing body meeting.

Minimum commitment and annual programme

Different members of each governing body can give varying degrees of commitment, including school visits. Some governors are fortunate enough to be able to get into the school on a regular basis; others can get in occasionally and some, with the best will in the world, can never get in during the working day because of their home or work commitments. There is a danger that the latter could be made to feel guilty if a minimum level of classroom visiting (such as one visit per governor per year) were imposed. On the other hand, it can be important to demonstrate a public commitment by the whole governing body to regular school and classroom visits.

Is there a way through this? One solution is to consider the idea of an *equivalent* minimum commitment. This means that a commitment, for example, to a half-day *equivalent* per term on behalf of the whole governing body, could be achieved by all. The *equivalent* means that an individual governor could visit for an hour on each of three days. Clearly piecemeal visits are not ideal but this flexibility might enfranchise all governors and allow for those who can do so to visit more regularly and for longer periods.

A programme of visits should be planned, and ideally spread fairly evenly across the year. It is advisable to allocate this responsibility to an individual governor in consultation with the head.

Monitoring and review

The policy should be monitored annually and adjusted as necessary at the first full governing body meeting of the academic year. The key question to be addressed is: Are we doing what we said we'd do? Staff could offer their views through the head.

The policy could subsequently be reviewed formally by the governing body at the first meeting of each academic year. The key questions here would be:

- Are our visits achieving the potential benefits we identified?
- Have there been any unexpected benefits?
- How can we make the policy and practice even better?

A formal recording of the policy and its approval is important. Two sample forms for feeding back on individual governor visits to the governing body are given on the following pages.

Visit report form: example 1

_____ SCHOOL

Name of governor:

Area (responsibility):

Date:

Staff visited:

Objectives of visit:

1.

2.

3.

Brief notes:

Three positive comments:

1.

2.

3.

Two questions:

1.

2.

Visit report form: example 2

Name of governor:

Class visited:

Date of visit:

Purpose of visit:

Governor's comments:

Teacher's comments:

Headteacher's comments:

Signed:

---------------------------------- Governor

---------------------------------- Class teacher

---------------------------------- Headteacher

7. OUR OWN PERFORMANCE AS A GOVERNING BODY

As with evaluating the effectiveness of the school, we need to start from what an effective governing body looks like. Ofsted has published a variety of descriptions over the years.

Governing Bodies and Effective Schools lists various features of an effective governing body, which are here turned into questions:

How good are we at:

- working as a team?
- developing a good relationship with the head?
- managing our time and delegating effectively?
- running effective meetings?
- knowing the school?
- training and development?

A sample inspection report in the *Handbook for Inspecting Nursery and Primary Schools*, 2000, describes the characteristics of an effective governing body:

- The governors contribute substantially to the effectiveness of the school.

- They have high levels of expertise and are very well organised and thorough in their approach.

- They are also open to new ideas and adapt quickly. This enables them to seize opportunities when they arise.

- They have trust in the headteacher but expect him to be fully accountable to them. They, in turn, account well to the parents of the school.

- The governors are active and keep themselves very well informed about what is going on in the school. They make regular visits and report back to meetings of the governing body.

In the latest Handbooks, Ofsted offers a seven-point scale with lists of criteria for judging how effective a governing body is. This is used as the basis for an approach to self-evaluation on page 53. So, there's no shortage of advice on what an effective governing body looks like. How, then, can we evaluate ourselves to see how effective we are?

Characteristics of effective governing bodies

Effective governing bodies have

- a full complement of governors

- an effective chairperson

- good attendance at meetings

- a wide range of expertise and experience

- additional governors (if used) chosen with care

- new governors inducted to their role

- open and honest relationships between governors and the headteacher.

Making It Better, Ofsted, 2001

APPROACHES TO SELF-EVALUATION

You will recall that Chapter 2 stressed the importance of the self-evaluation of the governing body taking place in the context of whole-school self-evaluation. Ofsted's forms S3 and S4 provide very helpful templates for this process but they are not the only tools available.

There are many toolkits, guidance booklets and different ready-made approaches to this task, so you really don't need to look too far to find something to suit your governing body. Your LEA can provide recommendations. You can choose to make the process as quick and simple as you like, or go for a more comprehensive approach which might involve several hours' work, often with an external facilitator. It may or may not have a cost, depending on the source.

Some of the commonly used approaches follow.

The effectiveness continuum

Lessons in Teamwork (Ofsted/Audit Commission, 1995) found that although most governing bodies were reasonably effective, those at either extreme of the arrow below were particularly ineffective. One quick governing body self-assessment is to get everyone to pinpoint on the arrow where they think the governing body sits. The ideal is to be in the middle, but that's not easy.

Uncritical supporters	Questioning but supportive	Confrontational
Ineffective	*Effective*	*Ineffective*

Risks	Risks
failure to monitor	*poor support*
failure to identify problems	*excludes "lay" governors*
difficult to criticise	*no partnership*
unclear decision making	*overlap of roles*

Having agreed where we are, we might need to move more to the right on the arrow, which is very common, or back towards the left–hand side, which is, fortunately, infrequent!

Strengths and areas for improvement

Pass around a form asking each governor to list what they perceive to be the governing body's three main strengths and areas for improvement. These can then be collated for a collective view. This is very good preparation for an Ofsted inspection, though you shouldn't leave it till then and it shouldn't be your main motivation.

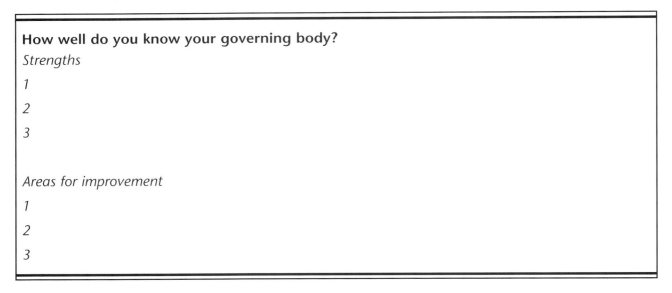

How well do you know your governing body?

Strengths

1

2

3

Areas for improvement

1

2

3

The follow up question is: "How do you know?", which can be difficult to answer, but if you're monitoring effectively, you should be able to come up with some reasonable evidence. You also need to know what the school is doing to address identified areas for improvement.

Again, you need to act on what you find.

Using *Governing Bodies and Effective Schools*

Take the six features of effectiveness listed in *Governing Bodies and Effective Schools* and break them down into smaller criteria, like this:

- **working as a team**
  attendance
  commitment
  using everyone's skills
  sharing the workload
  give and take
  respect
  loyalty

- **good relationship with the head**
  mutual understanding
  setting framework
  allowing head to manage

- **effective time management and delegation**
  prioritising
  delegating
  terms of reference
  reporting back

- **effective meetings**
  agendas reflecting priorities
  effective clerk
  purposeful chair
  clear minutes with action points
  outsider participation

- **knowing the school**
  organised co-operatively
  talking to pupils and staff
  visiting classrooms

- **training and development**
  taking development seriously
  identifying needs
  allocating funds
  courses, visits, on-site training.

Working independently of each other, award marks out of ten for each criterion according to how well you think your governing body meets it. Then compare results. This will help you get down to a finer level of detail than the first two approaches. It should help pinpoint some specific areas in which you need to improve.

Ofsted's seven-point scale

Simply look at the Ofsted scale for evaluating governing bodies, reproduced on the next page, and discuss where yours sits most comfortably.

Other forms of self-evaluation

As already said, there are many other approaches available, most of which are more sophisticated than any of the above. Your first port of call should be your local Governor Support Team who either will have a ready-made approach involving a training session with the whole governing body or will be able to lend you a self-evaluation pack. Some good examples are:

The Index of School Governance, written by Catherine Burt

The Governing Body Builder, Dorset LEA

The Effective Governing Body, Oxfordshire LEA.

Whatever approach you use, the important thing is what you do with what you find out. Inevitably, you'll need to write some kind of governing body development plan to address your areas for improvement. This can be identical in format to your school's improvement plan, and, indeed, should be incorporated in it. Don't try to do too much, though. Two to three main actions are all that most governing bodies will have time to address, and some things may take a while.

Apart from anything else, incorporating the governors' development in the SIP promotes governor involvement in the different stages of the school improvement planning process, which can provide very useful learning for individuals and the collective team. And it gives a very powerful message to the head, staff and parents: we're in this together!

Ofsted's seven-point scale of governance

Very Good (2) *Creativity and dynamism in reflecting upon performance, promoting change and capitalising on links with the local community suggest* ***Excellent (1)*** *governance*	The governing body makes a major contribution to the leadership of the school, including its sixth form and its successes. It is fully involved in strategic planning and formulating policies, and supports staff in implementing them. Governors keep in close touch with the school's work across all stages, and this cements the partnership between the governing body and the school. The pattern of the governing body's work meshes well with the school's development cycle, so that both are very influential. Governors are well aware of the school's strengths and weaknesses and deal with them openly and frankly, contributing fully to development planning. Performance management procedures are very effective and are monitored closely by the governing body.
Good (3)	The governing body influences the work of the school and its policies through challenge and support. It has a good grasp of the school's strengths and weaknesses and has a significant, strategic influence in leading the school's development, with a clear focus on raising standards and improving the quality of provision. The governing body is prepared to take difficult decisions where necessary. It is well organised and it improves its own performance through appropriate development activities or training.
Satisfactory (4)	The governing body ensures that the school meets its statutory responsibilities, and has clear aims and policies. Its performance management policy operates effectively. Corporately, it sets an overall direction for the school and formulates policies that reflect the individual character of the school. It reviews performance data to monitor the whole school's work and its recommendations for action are followed up. All governors understand their role and any specific responsibilities. There is a businesslike relationship between governors and senior staff in leading the school.
Unsatisfactory (5)	The school fails to meet one or more statutory responsibilities and lacks some of the policies that are required. The governing body relies too heavily on the headteacher. Although they are supportive, governors play a slight part in leading the school and do little to hold the school to account. The work lacks focus and influence. They have insufficient knowledge of one or more of the stages. There is little corporate agreement about the school's strengths and weaknesses. The governing body has a limited grasp of the performance of the school and only modest effect on its development.
Poor (6) *High vacancies, poor attendance, hostile relationships and almost total reliance on the headteacher are indications of* ***Very Poor (7)*** *governance*	Important statutory responsibilities are not met. The governing body is remote from the school. Relationships between members of the governing body or between it and the senior staff are at best indifferent and may be hostile or acrimonious. Governors' business is badly organised and their conduct presents a barrier to school improvement. Governors are largely unaware of the strengths and weaknesses of the school and, in particular, of the effectiveness or otherwise of its senior managers. They have limited influence on the work of the school. The governing body presents no challenge. Standards and quality are not assured and it fails to set a clear direction or priorities for the school's work.

CONCLUSION

At the beginning of this book I said, "With monitoring and evaluation there is a real danger that governors could try to monitor and evaluate everything that moves. And if so, they will inevitably fail. We have to think through what this means. We need to see that we should focus only on the core activities that add value to our contribution to the school. It may mean stopping doing some of the things we do now and certainly will mean not trying to do the impossible." Even after sifting to find the essentials of monitoring and evaluating, we're still left with a daunting list:

- school performance data
- policies and plans
- the budget
- the school (or learning) environment
- our own performance as a governing body.

But the list is not too bad if we realise that of the two activities, evaluation is much more important than monitoring, provided the staff we employ are doing their jobs properly. So if your confidence in the staff allows you to reduce the amount of unnecessary direct monitoring by governors as far as possible, that should help you refocus your energies. As we've seen, though, a minimum of direct monitoring will always be necessary, especially in relation to the budget.

Within the list above, some things will be more important to you in your school than others – and those priorities may well shift from one year to the next, depending on circumstances and events. Keeping them under review and not being afraid to say that for this coming year your main (but not exclusive) focus will be on evaluating the School Improvement Plan, for example, will help you do your job successfully. In the end, you have to judge these things for yourself and you always run the risk of taking your eye off the ball. But schools are encouraged to develop a risk-taking culture, so maybe the governors should join in too!

Another way to make sure you cope is to have the best possible systems and processes in place to manage all the tasks. Some evaluation is best done collectively, some by smaller groups, such as committees or task groups, and some by individuals. Sharing the workload effectively is vital – but what works this year may need to change next year, so stay flexible and be creative in seeking solutions.

As a governor, you get used to being asked to do the impossible. Being a successful governor means mastering the art of the possible – and not feeling guilty about the bits that didn't quite get done.

INDEX